A Day
OF
Change
MOVES THE HEART

Out of It Flow the Issues of Life
Proverbs 4:23

HELEN

A Day of Change Moves the Heart
Trilogy Christian Publishers
A Wholly Owned Subsidary of Trinity Broadcasting Network
2442 Michelle Drive
Tustin, CA 92780
Copyright © 2023 by Helen Elliott

For information, address Trilogy Christian Publishing
Rights Department, 2442 Michelle Drive, Tustin, CA 92780.
Trilogy Christian Publishing/ TBN and colophon are trademarks of Trinity Broadcasting Network.
For information about special discounts for bulk purchases, please contact Trilogy Christian Publishing.
Manufactured in the United States of America

10 9 8 7 6 5 4 3 2 1
Library of Congress Cataloging-in-Publication Data is available.
ISBN: 979-8-88738-395-8
ISBN: 979-8-88738-396-5

How Many Hats Are You Wearing?

Again, you have heard that it was said to those of ancient times, "You shall not swear falsely, but carry out the vows you have made to the Lord." But I say to you, do not swear at all, either by heaven, for it is the throne of God, or by the earth, for it is his footstool, or by Jerusalem, for it is the city of the great King. And do not swear by your head, for you cannot make one hair white or black. Let your word be "Yes, Yes" or "No, No;" anything more than this comes from the evil one.

Matthew 5:33-37 (NKJV)

In the Beginning

Redesigning your life everyday is *A Day of Change*

Do Not Be Afraid
Do Not Be Discouraged
Be Grateful
Be Loving
Sit, be still…
Listen to you!
And follow your Dream…
If I can do it
So can you….
I know it is hard to
Let go of our past…
When you do
you will feel freedom to
Love yourself
More each day…
I will be praying for you!
Trust yourself for
A Day of Change
To change your life!
Do it each day.
And God said let there be light!

Helen

SPECIAL ACKNOWLEDGMENT

I would like to give extra special thanks to my daughters for putting up with a mother who was growing up later in life.

Thank you also to my parents for always taking us to church.

Many thanks to Donna Wick, for her assistance with this book.

How do I say thank you to so many wonderful friends, speakers, ministers, authors, and of course my family, over the years they were all part of my education and growth throughout the years to learn all I could about our Lord, Jesus Christ. Blessings and many thanks to all of you and for the healing of my heart.

To my Spiritual Leader from above, Jesus.

Thank You,

Helen

TABLE OF CONTENTS

TODAY IS: A DAY OF CHANGE

Today, Father, I will long only for You. From the very depths of my heart, I shall seek you with all my heart, with all my soul and with all my mind.

I accept Your loving guidance in everything I do.

And in times when I do not understand, I will simply trust that You have watch over me and my heart.

My vow today is to keep close to You as You lead me forward to the destiny of my dreams. You have planted these dreams in the secret-most chambers of my heart and when the time is right, You will reveal all.

A DAY OF CHANGE

Because all the stories are true and most profound, this book promises to be the most different of all relationship books. Each day millions of men and women go online looking for love. Some are genuinely in earnest search while others troll for attention and flattery. The fact is, everyone wants love – we want to be loved and to have someone in our life to love. Love, and the sense of belonging, is an essential part of us that needs to be nurtured and honored.

We all have our histories of bad relationships and failed marriages. These are not things we brag about but rather things we try to learn from. Yet, most of us go right back into relationships that ring similar to the one we just left or survived.

This is what I know to be true. If we knew how to do things differently, we would. We don't go back into the same types of relationships because they are fun for us. We enter into the same type of relationships because we don't know any better how to pursue anything different. And this is why I wrote this book.

A Day of Change is about entering into a vow with God to lead us to the right person, the right relationship and at the right time. This book is about how to trust God so that we no longer have to spin and toil in a relationship that could possibly be hurtful, abusive or demoralizing all the while trying desperately to make it work. If God knows the count of every hair on our head, He knows the right person He has in mind for us to love us and to have us love back.

Every day we wake up and don't have to give a single thought as to how we will breathe throughout the day, how our organs will function or how many beats of our heart will be necessary for us to stay alive. No, God has done this for us. And yet, when it comes to matters of our life and of our heart, we feel that God could never understand or could never bring to us what we so desire. I must keep reminding myself of scripture wherein God says to us all, "Come to me all of you who are burdened and I will give you rest."

God led me out of this relationship and brought me back into His arms again. God was there for me – caring for me, loving me.

A Day of Change is about trusting God to lead us in all ways.

What is stopping me from trusting God? How has life been made better with you trying to work things out? I can rethink the power and authority of God in my life by

_____

_____

_____

_____

_____

_____

_____

_____

_____

_____

_____

_____

_____

_____

_____

Lord, You have heard the desire of the humble; You will prepare their heart; You will cause Your ear to hear.

Psalms 10:17 (NKJV)

YOU ARE LOVE

This world is a cold, bitter place when it comes to nurturing our spirit. It is up to us to redirect our thoughts and our focus. Daily advertisements tell us how much we are lacking. Everything is made to look better in that 30-60 second commercial span motivating yet another item for us to buy to get closer to the perfection this world fools us into thinking exists. But perfection does not exist in this world, but with our Father in Heaven.

Every day when we feel the pangs of getting closer to the supposed perfection of the world, we must realize that what is really happening within us is the call of our own soul to strive towards the perfection of our Lord. When I realized I was and could not be perfect nor did I have to be, the pressure subsided so that I could simply love me for me.

How we reach out to God is to love ourselves; a concept not made of this world. The world wants us unhappy with ourselves and to be in doubt about who we are and our own worth. But it is not "who we are" that matters but "whose we are." We are born of our Lord and every day we walk steeped in the love that gives us our next breath and that ensures the next beat of our heart.

Do not buy into the ways of this world. Do not look for perfection in this world. We were not created to live from the outside in, but from the inside out. So, we must daily nurture our spirit through tenderness. We must go inside and find the love of self so that we can walk with God and express His love through us. What a selfish thought I felt this was.

With a delicate, kind, and sweet spirit find God manifested beauty near flowers, sunlight, or anything pretty and beautiful no matter how sad you may feel. Every day take this time to love yourself, to nurture your spirit until you truly understand how wonderful you are. Love yourself so much so that all the pain you have been holding inside is diminished. It's your turn to love!

Who have you put before God and how is that
influencing your life?

_____

_____

_____

_____

_____

_____

_____

_____

_____

_____

_____

_____

_____

_____

*And I am certain that God, who began the
good work within you, will continue his work
until it is finally finished on the day when
Christ Jesus returns.*

Philippians 1:6 (NKJV)

LISTENING UP

There was a moment in my childhood when I was about two or three years of age, I was with my older brothers and sister at the farm. We had lost something near our stream that went through the field nearby and we knelt beside the stream and prayed to find the item we lost. Of course, we were told that praying would help us find what we lost, and it was then or from then that I began to believe in God.

A little defining moment served to interrupt my trust in God. We never found what it was we were looking for or at least I don't remember if we did. And most likely I walked away thinking they were right. I couldn't pray that God would help me find it.

Maybe I figured God was too important to look at my need or maybe that God was too busy. I am certain the person that told me prayer wasn't going to bring back the item most likely was not close with God and something so small is not important when you are two or three years old.

As I walk this world today, I still go back to that place that trusts God in everything. I now seek God in everything and isn't that what God wanted us to do. To love Him, seek Him and find Him in all that we make room for? Even as a small child I remember praying to Him every night before I fell asleep.

Don't let this world dissuade you. Remain convicted in God. He wants us to come to Him with every need we have; it tickles Him to know we trust Him that much.

The time I called on God that I can distinctively
remember Him answering me was when I

_____

_____

_____

_____

_____

_____

_____

_____

_____

_____

_____

_____

_____

_____

_____

*He comforts us in all our troubles so that we
can comfort others. When they are troubled,
we will be able to give them the same comfort
God has given us.*

2 Corinthians 1:4 (NKJV)

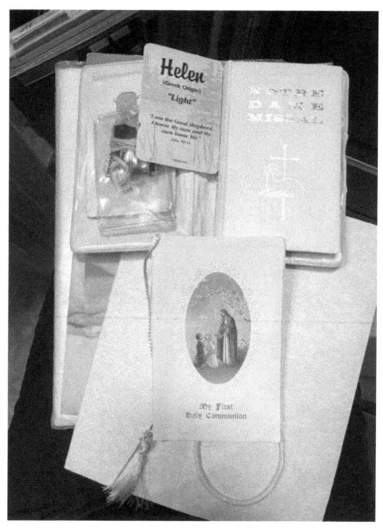

My First Communion

MY FIRST VOW

I can remember it as if it were yesterday. Pure and lovely, white and clean, there I stood ready to make my first vow at my first communion. I was incredibly happy, and I was innocent then though shortly later my innocence would be robbed of me. But on this day, oh, how I loved God. And to think of it, I always did love God. What happened to that time of innocence in Christ and that purity of joy?

How easy it is for one person to inflict a life-long battle of fear and insecurity to be dealt with. But through God and His Grace I was able to do so but not until much later in life. When we are young, the implications of being violated are not felt until we reach a time in our life where the pain begins to show. I never told anyone well into my forties what had happened to me. I was in denial for a very long time.

Maybe that is why people are so fearful of taking that first step in Christ. How could I after having made such a beautiful vow to God could God allow people to violate me? Maybe this is why people do not trust God to love them and care for them; to protect and guide them.

My only answer is that what happened to me was not of God, but of man. God did not violate me, man did. And it may be for one person to set us off on a road to destruction. I realized that God never turned His back on me. He was there to catch my first tear. I may not have realized it then, but God never left me.

As I grew up, I knew God was there to console me. I just did not understand to what degree. God always brought me back to where I needed to be.

Even as a child, I prayed for the person who violated me and as I did, I remember an overwhelming sense of peace and beauty came into my soul. I felt refreshed and vibrant. This could only happen through Grace.

Taking up a relationship with God has been like wrapping a big blanket around me. It will not stop the slings and arrows of this world, but it will be there soft and warm, ready to comfort me.

God cannot stop man from his behavior, but no matter the circumstance - God is already there, waiting for us on the other side. I can believe God is walking with me or waiting for me to reach out because

_____

_____

_____

_____

_____

_____

_____

_____

_____

_____

_____

_____

We know how much God loves us, and we have put our trust in his love. God is love, and all who live in love live in God, and God lives in them.

1 John 4:16 (NKJV)

HYPOCRITE

It didn't take me long to understand that guys like contact sports. They eagerly engage in sports like wrestling, football, boxing, and sex – yes, sex! I knew better though or should have. I thought the distance would impede a man's will to win in this way, but in the end it really didn't matter. I made the choice to engage never asking for God's advice our counsel.

Though the relationship was a long distance one, there were moments of togetherness and I realized that I was engaging in a contact sport of my own free will. And to be honest, I did enjoy that aspect of the relationship. I also realized that some men would do anything to win that game.

I have slipped at times in my vow with God to engage in such physical contact with men way before I had developed trust or even friendship. This is not an easy vow to make or keep.

I had to break through the fleshly desire and wait on God's choice for me and not my own. I came to the realization that going from one relationship to another made me feel worse not better.

At one point, I became appalled at myself. It brought me to my knees and the greatest pain I have ever experienced continuing to engage in sex after vowing to God I would not. I hurt deep in my heart so much because I had betrayed

God and myself.

The important thing to remember is that I keep coming back to my vow and this is what God wants to see of us most.

When I give myself away, I feel

_____

_____

_____

_____

_____

_____

_____

_____

_____

_____

_____

_____

_____

_____

_____

_____

God never changes his mind when he gives gifts or when he calls someone.

Romans 11:29 (NKJV)

My Childhood Diary

LOOKING FOR FOOD

As I sat by the ocean and watched the birds circle the sky then dive for food, I noticed some birds perched on trees, eating berries; some birds landed softy on dew covered grass, eating worms; and some birds hit the pavement, eating roadkill!

What fills me with wonder is that all are part of God's evolution.

Even the bird eating roadkill is part of evolution to eat what other birds will not even though we might find this repulsive. I know that God has a plan for both things beautiful and unsavory, because all are necessary.

I look at my life and think about the messy times and see clearly that because of my errors and ultimately my self-correction in Christ, my mistakes were necessary to deepen my commitment to my journey with God and my vow unto Him. He needs me to accomplish something for Him if I will just let Him do His work in me.

We look at our lives and see that there are times we have sat with "roadkill" in our relationships and peer groups, but from that we learned something. It was all part of our evolution. So, I do not judge myself on this, but I embrace the lesson learned. Instead of complaining, I listen for God's direction through the love of self and Him that He has instilled in me.

Through His wisdom I will reach my destiny.

I always know when I am off course because the peace seems to escape my sense. This is how we miss God. Because God is Peace and we do not realize when the peace leaves our life that basically He has stepped aside leaving us to our free will. It isn't that He left, but that we have turned our back on Him.

When we begin to feel the power of this world and we have lost our peace is when we need to sit and listen. Listen to God's world. To the sounds of nature and to the sound of His voice.

We must walk through this world, but we do not have to succumb to it. Like the quote reads, "Life is a bridge meant for crossing, not build a home on it." I continue to cross over my many bridges in life and each time walk with the compass of God in my heart and His peace in my spirit.

I can now see that the not-so-great times of my life were part of my evolution. Because of these experiences I am now.

_____

_____

_____

_____

_____

_____

_____

_____

_____

_____

_____

_____

_____

_____

_____

_____

_____

For in many things we all stumble.
James 3:2 (NKJV)

THE ENCOUNTER

There is nothing like exalted validation.

I remember after my ex-husband vehemently denied his affair, I ran in to him and his soon to be wife. In fact, they ran right into me at the courthouse counter applying for their marriage license. How crazy was that? And they applied for their marriage license close to thirty days after our divorce. Though he never admitted it to me, clearly, he had been having an affair. I had wanted validation and boy did I get it.

What I didn't expect was the pain I would feel seeing them together, hearing them laugh and seeming so happy.

Sometimes, God will allow things to hit us squarely between the eyes just so we can plainly see that our intuitions were correct and that we just did not trust ourselves with what we know. I will never second guess God again.

When God puts something in my heart, I will not question what it is or where it came from. I will simply trust. It's not about what I want to see or hear. It's about what God has to reveal to me. THAT is powerful!

The more I trust God, just as in a love relationship in this world, the deeper my commitment runs. To have a vow and relationship with God means to trust God with all your heart. The reason we do not trust God is that sometimes we don't really want to see the truth. We don't want to admit we've been wrong. We don't want the fun to stop.

But to take up a vow with our Lord means to trust everything He puts in our hearts and to trust that He has placed those feelings, those nudgings are there to protect our spirit, to protect our heart and to keep us on the path.

What it means to trust God is to trust that

_____

_____

_____

_____

_____

_____

_____

_____

_____

_____

_____

_____

_____

_____

_____

_____

_____

_____

I delight greatly in the LORD;
my soul rejoices in my God
Isaiah 61:10 (NKJV)

IT IS FINISHED

Going back to the time I saw my ex and his soon to be new wife applying for their marriage license shortly after our divorce, knowing then that though he never admitted to the affair, clearly there has been one. After seeing this right in front of my face I composed myself long enough to walk out to my car. Once inside I fell apart.

I cried from such a place of pain. He had made me feel like I was crazy to even suggest he was having an affair and yet, here he was clearly applying for a marriage license only days after our divorce. I couldn't deny the experience.

But as I cried, God spoke to me: You were the last one to know about the affair. Now you are the first one to know about the marriage.

The words were clear: "It Is Finished."

It's like the faucet was turned off. My tears subsided and God filled my heart with such a feeling of freedom. Yes, it was finished, and God took that pain and replaced it with upliftment and freedom. I thought, yes, now I know. God gave me validation that could not be disputed. A freedom I could not explain. I would not have to endure this pain again if I vowed to listen to Him and Him alone.

I was free in the revelation of what the truth was and from that moment I could walk on. The pain of the divorce and the lost relationship was real, but so was the freedom I felt in Christ. The blessing was that the freedom feeling grew while the sadness waned. This is the glory of my vow and relationship with God.

As God fed me that evening after that encounter, I felt so loved to have such a gift as validation in my heart. God truly was helping me heal. God also brought a friend of mine along who witnessed this from her car and who gave me comfort. God thought of everything. And yes, it was finally finished.

In the stillness, I know that God is

_____

_____

_____

_____

_____

_____

_____

_____

_____

_____

_____

_____

_____

_____

_____

_____

Therefore, when Jesus had received the sour wine, He said, "It is finished!" And He bowed His head and gave up His spirit.

John 19:30 (NKJV)

Looking to Soften Me Up

WINDOWS TO OUR SOUL

I look to the past and let go of all the pain and agony; both to the pain I caused and to what I experienced from childhood to the present day. It is a painful path, but necessary.

There are no reasons that can justify my pain. There is no apology great enough to soothe my inner wounds or those I caused others. But for me to assess my pain and to see things clearly is when I can begin to let it go. And this happens in my own time.

God is not rushing me to do this. What God does promise though is that when I am ready to look inside, He will renew and strengthen me. This is what comforts me on the journey. It has truly made being with our Lord so loving and kind. He hears me all the time. I can depend on Him.

What we must realize is that when we make a vow to God, God in turn makes a vow to us. He vows to love and heal us. God vows to support and encourage us. God vows to make new and set aright our direction in life.

What greater gift than the promise of our Lord's love, healing, and renewal?

We may think to take up a vow with God is to deny certain things in our life that we do not wish to give up. But what it really means is to let go of things that hurt us and cause us pain. And don't we want to let all that pain and suffering go? Don't we really wish to walk in step with God? Aren't we really seeking the peace and comfort of all God promises us?

To take up a vow with God means to free ourselves of the pain we have caused others. It isn't about judgment. It is about freedom.

Freedom to me means to feel like I am

_____

_____

_____

_____

_____

_____

_____

_____

_____

_____

_____

_____

_____

_____

_____

_____

_____

_____

_____

Remain in God's love.
Jude 1:2 (NKJV)

THE FINAL FRONTIER

I had entered my second marriage and thought that I had hit the Final Frontier. I thought I had found the happiness I had been seeking, yet happiness was more elusive than ever. I can honestly say that in this marriage there was such sadness. In fact, there were very few happy times.

I knew this was not the relationship God had in mind for me. I know I am not alone in sharing this experience. Many women and men have encountered the same plight as mine and are even still stuck in that negative, abusive, and mean-spirited relationships. I feel deeply for anyone who is not in a truly loving relationship, especially one with their parents or their spouse or with their children.

What I learned though is my first love is God and the relationship I should pursue is that of God. The more I looked to man for my love and acceptance, my validation and comfort – I would always be disappointed. Man cannot satiate the inner longing of my soul to be loved at that level. I had to learn to love me first. I had to stop looking for man and look to me.

Basically, we are all selfish creatures. We want to be loved and in the way we want that love to be shown. We go into relationships with a "what can you do for me" attitude instead of "how by loving me can your life be enriched." The world would look differently should the latter be the case. It is fun now helping others and enriching their lives. It is rewarding loving others along the way just as God loves me.

I never thought as myself as selfish, but I was selfish because how could I give to others and feel that great feeling of service when I could not give my time to the one who was most important – my God!

Our love with God is selfless and the most rewarding love we could ever experience. When I am pursuing a godly relationship with my Creator, my Creator is also at work to match me with a person who is just as godly.

Through my love of Christ, I am being groomed. It has been a painful but gift giving process.

I have discovered the qualities I am willing to give to
God in a love relationship and those that I was willing to
give to a natural relationship are best contrasted as

_____

_____

_____

_____

_____

_____

_____

_____

_____

_____

_____

_____

_____

_____

_____

_____

*For all seek their own, not the things which
are Jesus Christ's.*

Philippians 2:21 (NKJV)

The Secret . . . I Was So Young!

THE SECRET

There are defining moments in my life that I can clearly see the genesis of destruction and the havoc I created. It isn't pretty, but I am clear on how and why certain things evolved in my life.

When I was young, I was sexually molested. Just that sentence alone seems to be so overused which hurts my heart really. So many of us, men and women alike, have been physically, emotionally, or sexually abused. And for every unique experience there is an equally unique response as to how to handle that trauma. For me, I was promiscuous and had an affair in my first marriage. I don't revel in this admission. I brought so much pain to so many. I can never undo what wrongs I have done.

I share this to say that though I can clearly look back and grieve my actions. I also understand that I was doing the best that I could at the time with the resources I had. I even attended church through all of this.

There is no perfect way or "right" way for us to anesthetize our pain and grief. All we can do is all we can do and even writing that I feel like in a way that is a cop-out, but it isn't. I may not understand someone's actions or choices in life. It is easy to sit and judge. But my experiences taught me that people do unacceptable things in trying to move away from their own pain and trauma.

I also was trying to move away from my pain and in doing so, caused much pain to others. This is when The vow with Christ is so important because He sees my heart when others cannot. Christ knows that what I did was not intentional to harm or injure others. Christ knows what I was trying to do. But He could not get through to me. What I didn't appreciate was that each relationship pummeled me deeper into the abyss of hell. I wanted out but didn't know how to do so.

If only I would have followed the vow I made as a child to wait on God! Yet, how could I have known. I started early on making my own choices and it finally brought me to my knees thirty-five years later!

So, the secret is, I was scared early on, but God can move us away from the pain of our past as we enter into a loving relationship with Him. It took me a long time to understand that God was the total answer!

As I ask forgiveness, forgiveness is given
and that makes me feel

_____

_____

_____

_____

_____

_____

_____

_____

_____

_____

_____

_____

_____

_____

_____

The Lord is good and does what is right; He
shows the proper path to those who go astray.
Psalms 25:8 (NKJV)

THE TRAP

What little girl or little boy doesn't dream of a future love and a life of happiness. It seems that we are "wired" to wish for this. I was no different. I wanted a life with my prince charming and to feel loved. Just to hear those words, "I love you" were so deeply sought.

It was my passion to find passion if you know what I mean. I knew the passion was strong inside of me because God kept reassuring me in my prayers and in how I felt. But I didn't listen after prayer time, I simply went right back to making the first move away from Him.

What I didn't realize was how needy and clingy I was to that passion. I was drawn to do anything I could to feel that feeling and to hear those words. When I did finally hear them, I was sucked in like a fleck of dust to a filter. He was truly a silver-tongued devil. And in the end, I was trapped. I was trapped by the very words and feelings I most desired.

I wanted to feel love and to feel wanted, loveable and desired. I wanted my Knight in Shining Armor. I sold out to natural love. Today I passionately love God and self and freely give the love and passion that was given to me. My prayer is to be able to one day freely love 'the one' God has in mind for me.

Now that I am open and receptive to the love of God, I feel I can almost hear the hearts of others as I get to know them because my heart is so open.

God's love is not stifling or abusive. God's love is not conditional or wavering. God's love is all in all. His love is everything to me now. I am relaxed in God's love and comforted in His Grace and Comfort. I take and share with him all day knowing I cannot do it alone.

God loves me with all His heart, and I truly learned how to love through Him. I learned to give God my faith and my trust. I now allow God to take my hand and heal my heart.

I know no trap with God and because I walk with God, I feel He spares me traps from others. I am not saying that my heart will never be broken, but I am not going into relationships as needy as I was before because I am satiated in God's love for me.

In God I have no fear to trust,
to believe which means I can

_____

_____

_____

_____

_____

_____

_____

_____

_____

_____

_____

_____

_____

_____

_____

*Peace I leave with you; my peace I give you.
I do not give to you as the world gives. Do
not let your hearts be troubled and do not be
afraid.*

John 14:27 (NKJV)

My Quiet Place . . . Beside Still Waters

LEAD ME TO STILL WATERS

Psalm 23 traverses through my heart like a country creek across the terrain. It is easy and nurturing. It is how God means for us to live without worry or anxiety.

I remember the day I felt that kind of comfort. It was the day I found my home. Driving over a small hill there it was. Perched on a small lake surrounded by trees, there stood the perfect Bed & Breakfast type cottage. I knew this was where I could fully renew. I knew this was where God wanted me to be.

I had been looking for a new home but hadn't found anything that I truly just loved. Maybe looking for a home was a lot like looking for a romance in my life. I looked here and there and never found what truly suited me. Then one day, driving around, I crested a hill and there it was. I suppose it is true that we will find what we are looking for when God is ready to reveal it to us and when we ready to have it revealed.

Walking around the outside of the house with my friend, but not having seen the inside of this house or assessed the amenities, I knew it was mine. I knew this was my house! And then, as God promised, He took the steps as He vowed to bring deeply into my heart what He finally wanted for me. He wanted to give me rest. He wanted to give me deep, abiding peace. He wanted to lead me beside still waters.

This was a God-ordained journey. God delivered me to my home. And what I walked away from this experience is to know that God is only too willing to deliver me in all things and in all ways. We are the ones who stress and struggle. We are the ones that make life so complicated and frustrating.

God will lead us to still waters.

Realizing that God is alive and well and at
work in the lives of every living creature,
I find comfort by remembering

_____

_____

_____

_____

_____

_____

_____

_____

_____

_____

_____

_____

_____

_____

_____

_____

He maketh me to lie down in green pastures:
He leadeth me beside still waters.
Psalms 23:2 (NKJV)

VALIDATION

I could write pages and pages on this. We all want validation. We want to know that we did or said the right thing or if when things fall apart, others are there to affirm they would have done the same thing.

I'm reminded of an old Yellow Pages ad: "let your fingers do the walking" and boy mine sure did. They did more than walk. My fingers ran across the dial pad so fast it would have made your head spin. I would call everyone to affirm my decisions or to cast my cares to them. The only thing is that this only served to hang new drapes, so to speak, in the same old house.

I simply could not find enough people on which to vomit all my pain. I hurt so much inside. Finally, and thankfully, I just stopped. I was just so tired. There was no longer any satisfaction from spewing my pain, my hurt, my disappointment on others. I was tired of it all and I am sure they were as well.

I went deep into my cave (my new home) and Jesus began to teach me His words because I was finally ready to listen.

Only God can lift us up. Only God can take away our pain. Only God can comfort our heart and restore our soul. Only God can take our pain and instill peace to our mind and spirit.

It might feel like the thing to do to call upon friends and family to share your side of a situation because all that is 'real time.' We feel like we are being productive. We feel like calling everyone is making progress. But truly, only God can give us peace and solace to the tribulations of this world.

I am more particular about who I ask advice from now. Instead of calling on everybody and heeding their opinions and counsel, I now look to God. I lift up my cares and He sends down the blessings. And He is always right.

His words – His vows, are there to protect and care for me. When I stopped talking is when my life really started to change. I would sit and listen to God's guidance and advice brought huge clarification to me.

VALIDATION

My friends are wonderful,
but when I call on God I know

_____

_____

_____

_____

_____

_____

_____

_____

_____

_____

_____

_____

_____

*Then Jesus said, "Come to me, all of you who
are weary and carry heavy burdens, and I
will give you rest."*

Matthew 11:28 (NKJV)

71

OMNISCIENT GOD

If you are physically ill, you need to make an appointment with your doctor. If you are emotionally distraught, you need to make an appointment with your therapist. And if you need the company of friends, you have to get on their calendar. All these are delays to the help you need and need right now!

One of the amazing things of God is that God doesn't require a reservation. God does not require an appointment, or for us to take a number and sit down or even to write our name on the tablet to be called when He is available. No, the wondrous nature of our omniscient God is that He is always here and always available for our every situation.

Have you ever really thought about that? Have you ever thought about how available He is to us? How in the world does He have time for me and everyone simultaneously?

God is God.

His vow is to always be available at any time. No restrictions.

Just think how we would feel to know we had a physician on call 24 hours a day, 7 days a week, 365 days a year. We would brag till the sun sets about having this type of availability.

Yet, we take God's availability for granted or dismiss it altogether. Why? Because we don't believe it can happen for us. We don't truly believe that He works for us. All we have to do is just listen!

I have learned the hard way, but still I have learned. When I am in need, I only need to sit and reflect on the wondrous glory of God and how He is always here when I need Him. In an instant, God is accessible in our lives. Every corner we turn He is right there to lead us even if we didn't listen and missed it. If we come back, He will try again and again.

I am learning to listen or at least try to find the time to ask for assistance. I have wasted too many years doing it on my own.

When I am still and quiet God is able to

_____

_____

_____

_____

_____

_____

_____

_____

_____

_____

_____

_____

_____

_____

_____

Have you not known? Hast thou not known?
Has thou not heard the earth, fainteth neither
is weary? There is no searching of his
understanding.

Isaiah 40:28 (NKJV)

FIGHTING BACK

It is easy to get in a rut of doing the same things over and over again yet expecting some different result to manifest. This is the definition of insanity. You feel it from the mundane chores of your life to the larger, life-changing occurrences. Like losing your keys. If we don't focus on placing our keys in a set place when we walk into our home at night, then we are guaranteed to search like crazy mad for them the next day. That's insane. We must focus and prepare a place. We must define a strategy so that we are not always chasing our tail!

I was "loving insanely" meaning, I was doing the same things over and over again in my relationships and expecting different results. No wonder they never changed. They only would be worse each time. I had no strategy.

So there has to be a point in time when your internal system screams "Abort – Get Out – Listen to Your Gut." There has to be that moment when you think, "Stop it. Just stop it!"

The problem is we rarely heed our internal warning mechanisms to keep ourselves safe and free from hurt, confusion or frustration.

This is why daily prayers and reflections are so very important because this is the time, we connect with God so that when those warnings go off, we realize that we are "listening to our gut" as intuition – as the very voice of God.

I know you have been there when all systems are saying to get away from a particular person or situation and yet we continue to move deeper into the abyss of emotional chaos.

The way we "fight back" and take control of our lives is to daily pray, meditate, and reflect on the Word of God so that when the warnings come, we know who sent them and to ask for help.

I have experienced going down the wrong road
and had I truly heeded the Word of God
I could easily have avoided

Pray without ceasing.
1 Thessalonians 5:17 (NKJV)

WALKING A NEW WAY

There is an expression that states, "you've made your bed now lie in it" and I understand what that means is to take responsibility for one's actions. What it does not mean is for us to wallow in the mire of our past mistakes. Everyone makes mistakes. Every one of us is flawed.

Have you ever gone through a stage in your life where you didn't think you were flawed? Ha! I did. But God clearly showed me that I was 'perfectly imperfect' and that I did not have to lie in-state of my failings and transgressions. This is not what God wants for us. It certainly didn't make me feel good, but I needed to know.

To take up a vow with God means to do a new thing in one's life and to begin again in a new relationship with Him– to make a new bed essentially. Hopefully, a gorgeous flower bed with new beautiful flowers like you have never seen!

I remember starting over and how I actually began to walk a new way. I held my shoulders back and kept my head up. At times I felt awful, but God led me to do this for Him if I followed His word. I cleaned up and focused on looking good for God. This was very empowering for me because I felt the change inside and out. I was wearing my change in life! And being me was actually a relief.

God does not want us to live a life of martyrdom for our

sins. God wants us to rise above our sins of the past. God wants us to "rise and walk"! God gives us the strength we need to do this. This is why it is essential to listen to His words.

There may be those around you that will want to remind you of your failings, misgivings and transgressions of the past. They may even speak ill of you. You must walk away from those people. God does not want that for you.

Leave those that drag you down behind or you will re-live your past. They will take you a step back not forward. Pray for them. Forgive them. Find a new path, hold your head high and walk a new way.

To forgive myself means I can finally

And God shall wipe away all tears from their eyes; and there shall be no more death, neither sorrow, nor crying, neither shall there be any more pain: for the former things are passed away.

Revelation 21:4 (NKJV)

Be Still

PAUSE

We have an interesting way of praying. Think of prayer like a conversation and imagine yourself speaking to one of your friends. Imagine that you are sitting there telling them this and that and the other about your life. They may even know of the things you speak of but there you go going on and on about what hurts you, what caused you heartache, what frustrated or confused you. Now imagine that person just sitting there patiently listening to everything you have to say. And then, when finished, you just get up and walk off. Can you imagine their pain and feelings of rejection?

What do you think your friend would do? They would feel sad. They would feel invalidated. They would grieve that you left them in such a state.

Wouldn't they be calling out to you to wait a minute, to sit back down and to listen to what their thoughts were for you? Of course! Your friend would have some input. They would have some ideas on how to help you. But you are long gone!

Can you imagine that this might be how God feels when we pray?

We sit down and tell God everything yet fail to sit, pause and listen to what input God has for us. And it may not come in that very moment, but by pausing and sitting still for just a few moments, we are inviting God to be more active in our life. It might be during the day that the still small voice of God will be heard. It might be a flashing thought or an inspired moment or perhaps when we awake during the night just so He has our full attention.

The closer I get to Him the more my prayers are heard and the more content my life – if I will just sit still!

When I listen for the voice of God I feel

_____

_____

_____

_____

_____

_____

_____

_____

_____

_____

_____

_____

_____

_____

_____

_____

_____

Wisdom resteth in the heart of him that hath understanding.

Proverbs 14:33 (NKJV)

SEEDS OF HOPE

Hope is all around us, yet we feel so discouraged at times. We must pick up the seeds of hope as God sprinkles them throughout our day. I used to hope for this thing or that thing. Now I prefer God to lead me. I prefer God sprinkle seeds of hope in my relationships and on my path.

I gather seeds of hope when singing songs in church or when I meet up with a friend and experience their words of encouragement or encourage them. I hope I am also what they need as a seed of light and not a bringer of despair. I plant seeds of hope when I help a friend or do volunteer work or when I am in my women's prayer group or with my family.

Hope is all around, but we must look for it. Thankfully, God reveals evidence of hope through the birds in the trees, the creeks that flow, the shining sun and the luminescent stars at night. All of these seed His promise of hope for us.

It is easy to find what is discouraging and disappointing. It doesn't take a mental giant to conjure up doom and gloom. But to find hope, well that is an inspired person. That is a person of God.

I prayed and hoped for God to help me though so many rough times. My guilt, shame and feelings of unworthiness overcame me. I wanted to go home with Him. It would have been easier because the despair and the shame I carried was far too heavy for me to bear – or so I thought. What I really needed then, as I do today, is the hope of God in my life.

I need His help and His hope in my job, my relationships, with my children and through reconciling my divorce.

God has heard my prayers. I have a forever hope in God.

When I see that God is so much larger than myself and
acknowledge the evidence of God all around me I

_____

_____

_____

_____

_____

_____

_____

_____

_____

_____

_____

_____

_____

_____

_____

*May the God of endurance and encouragement
grant you to live in such harmony with one
another, in accord with Christ Jesus.*

Romans 15:5 (NKJV)

THE BLIND DATE

Everyone we meet is essentially a Blind Date. We are blind to their past. We are blind to their thoughts. We are blind to their agenda. And we are blind to their heart. What we must realize they are also blind to our thoughts, feelings, and intentions.

I dated someone for many years and did not know him. What I did know was that our beliefs were very different, and it was emotionally and physically hurtful to stay in that relationship. I knew this was not what God wanted for me. It was extremely hard for me to leave that relationship and the familiarity of our routine. It hurt more than I had anticipated, but I kept going through the pain. I remember wishing he could be my knight in shining armor to rescue me from my pain.

But how did things go so wrong? I know many people who have asked the same question of themselves, but who are we to know? There is no way we can know a person through and through. Only God can have that type of knowing. I didn't even know myself. How could I truly know the heart of another when I was so disconnected from myself. At the time I was even too tired to look up. If I would have, life would have been so much better a long time ago!

This is why it is so important to take up our vow and relationship with God every day. We must put on the yoke of surrender to the Wisdom and the Ways and the Word of God. I cannot know what is in someone's heart. I can listen to what they say and I can evaluate how I feel, but I cannot truly know how they feel. Only God knows. I used to think I knew everyone. How could I since I refused to know me?

So I may be blind to the history and the heart of another, but my eyes are open unto God. To take up the vow means to set our sights on God every day for clarity of purpose and our sense of direction.

Many times, I would forget to put God first and soon my life would begin to go awry. Each time I would muster more focus towards God until my life got back on track.

I no longer feel blind to what God wishes for me. I just have to slow down long enough to see and hear what it is He is telling me, and not forget my vow.

When I surrender to God, I find that

_____
_____
_____
_____
_____
_____
_____
_____
_____
_____
_____
_____
_____
_____
_____
_____
_____
_____
_____
_____

Love one another earnestly from a pure heart.
1 Peter 1:22 (NKJV)

ERASING THE PAST

Living in the world today is so very different from the days of the disciples. How I would have loved to have followed Jesus and to walk the shores of Galilee with Him. Wow, what wisdom!

But today we walk around with "gods" of this world. We walk with our iPhones, our iPads, all the technology that both serves us and scars us. We value our food, our clothing, our appointments and amenities, our friends, our life and yet, we leave behind the One that gives our life sustenance and substance.

In making the vow to walk with God I had to reposition my priorities from the "god" of my relationship to someone who was not good for me back to the God that gives me life.

I had to let go of my attachment to the reminders of this relationship which meant I had to erase all the hateful emails and all the hurtful text messages and voice mails that ensued over the course of time. How could I ever be free if I carried these reminders of him in this way?

So, I went on a quest to give up all the old once and for all. I knew it would not be easy. In the beginning I was very needy, and I did not want to let go for fear of the unknown. Would I ever find someone else again? Would I be alone? Would God fill my heart with such love that I would not be reminded of the love I lost?

I totally cleansed myself of this relationship, trashing cards, gifts, letters, furniture – all the reminders of him in my life. I truly wanted to be free and to start over in God. I knew this is who I wanted to be 100 percent. And oh my, did He ever show me the way!

God has big plans for you, but He can't make Himself known if we are carrying reminders of our past. We are truly dragging around our dead horses behind us with all our technology and sentimental mementos of conditional natural love. Every day God is trying to demonstrate His unconditional, supernatural love for us while we try to perform a Lazarus on our past loveless relationships.

Erase the past and move on. Move towards God and He will move you towards your dream.

Love your new freedom God has given you. Give yourself permission to live the life God has in store for you. What a concept! To love and trust God that much!

I know I am free when I can

_____

_____

_____

_____

_____

_____

_____

_____

_____

_____

_____

_____

_____

_____

_____

And the child grew and became strong; he was filled with wisdom, and the grace of God was upon him.

Luke 2:40 (NKJV)

A WOMAN'S WALK IS NEVER DONE

It is so interesting that with all the time saving devices we have today, we seem to be no further ahead. I think with the invention of devices like the microwave, the intention was for to have that extra time to spend with our family and children or have quiet time with God. Instead, we have just busied ourselves with even more things to do or devices to maintain like Facebook, iPhones etc. instead of being with family.

When we feel overwhelmed, we might want to first look at where we are responsible in the creation of our "busy-ness." Maybe we haven't made ourselves or our path the priority.

When we feel like a woman's walk is never done, then it is time to close our eyes and remember who we are and whose we are and to focus on our inner self than the outer world.

In this world of technology, truly the only device I need is that of the Holy Spirit as I am continually rejoined with God and remember that God is the only "device" I need to make it in this world – to transition beyond this world! Ha! And no batteries needed! God is like the ultimate Wi-Fi – I am always connected!

I know I am centered when I can

_____

_____

_____

_____

_____

_____

_____

_____

_____

_____

_____

_____

_____

_____

_____

_____

_____

_____

*Do not neglect your gift, which was given you
through a prophetic message when the body
of elders laid their hands on you.*

Timothy 4:14 (NKJV)

MY PEARL

After my divorce, I had an incredible desire to have a white kitten and God brought me Pearl. Pearl taught me to be tender and kind and soft. I realized through loving her that I did not need to be a tough person or a strict person or even a powerful person. That wasn't what Pearl loved about me. What Pearl loved was my essence not my persona. She just loved ME!

When I realized that she accepted me as I was, I felt that sharing more of that authentic self with her and the world. Do you know what happened? The world responded in kind. My friends and acquaintances began appreciating me for my kindness and my softness and my gentleness. They didn't need to know I was tough or powerful. They only wanted to get to know the soft side of me that I had hidden away so well. It felt great!

When we feel we need to prove a point, when we feel that we need to exercise our power and thrust our weight around that should be a great clue that we are operating from our ego and not our essence. It is okay to let go of the bravado to embrace the blessing of who and what we are.

I kept my kind, soft and gentle side from being with me all the time. I didn't want to reveal that side of me because it is my most vulnerable side. But that is why God sent me Pearl. Every day as I brushed her and took care of her,

I was reminded that this is the way God loves us. Every day He is nurturing us, loving us, and holding us in His gentle embrace. I can let go because I know God is there to hold me.

Just as I would never let any harm come to Pearl, God will not let any harm come to me.

I can remind myself anytime that I am soft, I am gentle,
I am loveable which makes me feel like

_____

_____

_____

_____

_____

_____

_____

_____

_____

_____

_____

_____

_____

And be not conformed to this world: but be transformed by the renewing of your mind, that you may prove what is that good, and acceptable, and perfect, will of God.

Romans 12:2 (NKJV)

FALLING INTO THE ARMS OF GOD

When my husband told me he wanted a divorce I completely lost it! We have all had those moments in life when we are completely submitted on the floor. That's where I found myself. I was on the floor virtually writhing in pain and hurt. And then I felt it – the arms of God.

I remember feeling like I wanted to die. I felt so hopeless. Everything was dark. I asked God to just take me. But then, I felt His arms around me and in my heart I could hear the words "I will not let anyone hurt you again. I will take care of you." I knew in that moment that God would never leave me. His words reassured me that He would never let me go and that I was important to Him.

Sometimes, I imagine just free-falling into the arms of God because I know He is there to catch me. I am not saying that God is always there to clean up our messes, but God is always there to love and comfort us and really, in the end, isn't that what we all long for to be loved, comforted, and cherished?

I'm so glad that I found God to be my friend and my comforter. I knew God would always be there with me from that moment on. The floor is where I found my deeper relationship with God as I had nowhere else to go. Now I stand with God.

Thinking about falling into the arms of
God makes me realize that

*And it shall come to pass in the day that the
Lord shall give thee rest from thy sorrow, and
from thy fear, and from the hard bondage
wherein thou wast made to serve.*

Isaiah 14:3 (NKJV)

EXPERIENCE THE MOMENT

Life is busy. I don't need to really tell you that, but then again, the reminder might serve us both well. The thing is, we get so very busy that we do not experience life in real time. We are either thinking of the past or the future. In fact, either we are regretting something in the past or panicking about the future. What good does that do us?

I had to stop running! I had already lost the race!

So, I came up with a saying, "Stay Here and Listen." It's simple but it reminds me that wherever I am, to be fully present and be mindful of what is going on around me. *Stay Here and Listen.*

I can't say this is how I stay, but I stay less "out there" than ever before. I am not living in the past or projecting into the future. I am here – all here.

When I slip, I can feel the anxious side of me begin to return. I can now recognize how that part of me feels and I can quickly get myself back to where I need to be – with God!

Praise God that He is so forgiving and that we can connect, disconnect and reconnect over and over again. We will slip. We will stray from God. We will try things on our own. But then when we are filled with anxiety and are in need of comfort, He is standing by ready to receive us again.

When I pay attention and am fully present
I begin to appreciate

_____

_____

_____

_____

_____

_____

_____

_____

_____

_____

_____

_____

_____

_____

_____

_____

*I meditate on all that you have done; I ponder
the work of your hands.*

Psalms 143:5 (NKJV)

HAVING YOUR HOUSE IN ORDER

A lesson that not many of us want to learn is to have our house in order. And, unfortunately, it does not mean to have your home clean and tidy, though that is important. It means to have your heart in order, the dwelling of the living Christ in order.

If you are thinking negative thoughts, do you really feel God wants to dwell there? If you are thinking jealous thoughts, deceitful thoughts, vengeful thoughts – why would our God want to burrow there?

Would we want to spend the night in a home that was filthy? Of course not. And when we think such ungodly thoughts, we are creating a toxic and nasty environment for our God to dwell.

To get my house in order has not been an easy process. My house, my heart, was a mess to be honest. For the longest time I rationalized that holding onto something was better than holding onto nothing – even it if meant holding onto the pain and suffering of the past. But little by little my heart is clear and now I am truly becoming the woman God created me to be.

Having our house in order is to make clean our actions and words and thoughts. Having our house in order is to be tidy from the inside out and to be accountable for the sanctuary of our God in us.

To have my house in order makes me feel like God is

_____

_____

_____

_____

_____

_____

_____

_____

_____

_____

_____

_____

_____

_____

_____

_____

He did not need man's testimony about man,
for he knew what was in a man.

John 2:25 (NKJV)

BRAIN TUMOR

For some of us it takes a life altering situation for us to realize the value of life. For me it was being diagnosed with a brain tumor when my daughter was but a toddler. I remember thinking that I might not ever see my daughter grow up and another woman would raise my daughter. I was riddled in fear that I would not be there for her in life, but at the same time, I was not afraid to die.

So, I made a deal with God that if He would heal me, I would dedicate my life to taking care of people for Him on earth. I formed elaborate prayers and pleas for God to heal me and to see the sincerity in my heart to turn my life for the good and the glory of God.

The thing about making deals with God is to ultimately realize that the deal IS God. That God is the goal. We don't need to earn our favor, we do not need to earn our love, we do not need to earn our healing with God. God decides and we submit.

Some may think that this is taking the easy way out. They do not see how God can move in a person's life and how one can be wholly focused on the Will of God.

I had to learn the hard way that God does not make deals. His love is unconditional. I had to learn that my love should be given to Him in the same way. Love is not a contest with points won or lost. Love is gentle, faithful, kind, and unconditional.

God waited a long time for me to come around to giving my love and faithfulness to Him. He did spare my life and He did give me the opportunity to be there for my daughter and to accomplish other things in life He had planned for me. I think I had to be willing though to simply let go and "die" to the way I had been doing things.

The issue is never the circumstance. The issue is always our trust and faith in God.

When I submit to God and trust in His ways,
I am free from

_____

_____

_____

_____

_____

_____

_____

_____

_____

_____

_____

_____

_____

*These things I have spoken to you, that in me
you might have peace. In the world you shall
have tribulation: but be of good cheer; I have
overcome the world.*

John 16:33 (NKJV)

REASON VS. VOW

We do not need a reason to follow God and His plan for our life. The vow is enough. This is our opportunity to say to God that I am here, and I am following in Your ways. Our ways got us in the predicaments in which we have found ourselves in time and again. His ways are righteous and loving.

A Day of Change is to follow God. To trust God. To believe that God has the best in store for us. We don't need a reason to trust and believe in this way. We don't need a reason to figure out why God would want to direct our steps. God just does. God loves us and wants the best for us. Reasoning and justification have nothing to do with it at all.

A Day of Change is to be obedient to God and sometimes in our ego we want to reason why we don't need to submit to God. We justify our actions.

Best that we take up the mantle of our vow and walk with God. His ways are far superior to what we might have in mind.

My vow to God came as a result from me giving myself away to earthly man in hopes of finding the love of my life. I realized that God was my one and only. My vow became to save myself for a marriage made in Heaven. And I may not have any idea how this will happen, yet, I know to wait for God in the meantime. He knows the desires of my heart and more importantly, He knows who is best and right for me.

My job in the meantime is to wait on God. My job, my vow, is to simply love God with all my heart. This vow has brought me so close to God though it felt like a lifetime of letting go to get here.

My thinking mind will try to rationalize my relationship with God and worse, to rationalize unfit relationships with men. My rational mind knows nothing of the divinity within me. My rational mind knows nothing of the plan God has in store for me.

My vow with God is to

_____

_____

_____

_____

_____

_____

_____

_____

_____

_____

_____

_____

_____

_____

_____

_____

_____

_____

_____

I will have compassion on you.
Isaiah 54:8 (NKJV)

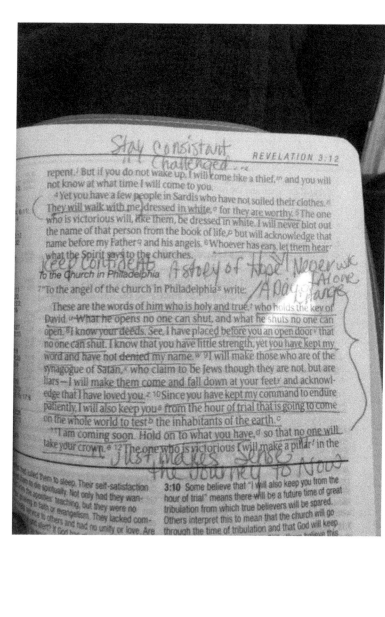

Stay consistint

Challenged...

repent.¹ But if you do not wake up, I will come like a thief,ᵐ and you will not know at what time I will come to you.

⁴ Yet you have a few people in Sardis who have not soiled their clothes.ⁿ They will walk with me, dressed in white,ᵒ for they are worthy. ⁵ The one who is victorious will, like them, be dressed in white. I will never blot out the name of that person from the book of life,ᵖ but will acknowledge that name before my Fatherᑫ and his angels. ⁶ Whoever has ears, let them hearʳ what the Spirit says to the churches.

Keep confident

To the Church in Philadelphia

A story of Hope | Never wk | Alone | A Day of change

⁷ "To the angel of the church in Philadelphiaˢ write:

These are the words of him who is holy and true,ᵗ who holds the key of David.ᵘ What he opens no one can shut, and what he shuts no one can open. ⁸ I know your deeds. See, I have placed before you an open doorᵛ that no one can shut. I know that you have little strength, yet you have kept my word and have not denied my name.ʷ ⁹ I will make those who are of the synagogue of Satan,ˣ who claim to be Jews though they are not, but are liars—I will make them come and fall down at your feetʸ and acknowledge that I have loved you.ᶻ ¹⁰ Since you have kept my command to endure patiently, I will also keep youᵃ from the hour of trial that is going to come on the whole world to testᵇ the inhabitants of the earth.ᶜ

¹¹ "I am coming soon. Hold on to what you have,ᵈ so that no one will take your crown.ᵉ ¹² The one who is victorious I will make a pillarᶠ in the

Just makes Sense

The Journey to Now

[them] to sleep. Their self-satisfaction [with] die spiritually. Not only had they wan- [dered from the] apostles' teaching, but they were no [longer growing] in faith or evangelism. They lacked com- [mitment] service to others and had no unity or love. Are [you alert]? If God has...

3:10 Some believe that "I will also keep you from the hour of trial" means there will be a future time of great tribulation from which true believers will be spared. Others interpret this to mean that the church will go through the time of tribulation and that God will keep [... them believe this]

THE WORD

As God began to renew my mind, I found I was on a path of wanting nothing more than to be with and learn about God. I began to feel much empowered. I couldn't believe what the Word was telling me about all my problems and my future. All of this wisdom I was learning coming from His Word from right in the palm of my hands!

Daily God takes me to college – His college of Wisdom, Righteousness, and Understanding.

For so many years I read every type of spiritual and religious book I could get my hands on. I went from book to book, tape to tape, CD to CD and church to church – all in search of the wisdom of God. What I do understand now of all the information I have received; the Bible is my book of choice. God sent me on a journey of Truth. He knew I would understand what He had been trying to tell me when I was finally ready to listen and all through His Word.

What is the worth of man's wisdom compared to the Wisdom of God? The Bible is still the most amazing book for me.

I can hardly wait each day to take up my Bible and receive the Word, the instructions for my day and the right answer for my worries.

I do not need to figure out everything on my own. It isn't up to me. It is up to God.

What is up to me is that I do my due diligence and immerse myself in the living waters of His Word and His Favor in my life.

This is one less worry for me.

I find my answer in the Word because

_____

_____

_____

_____

_____

_____

_____

_____

_____

_____

_____

_____

_____

_____

_____

_____

_____

And be not conformed to this world: but be ye transformed by the renewing of your mind, that ye may prove what is that good, and acceptable, and perfect, will of God.

Romans 12:2 (NKJV)

LIVING WITH GOD

There is a story in the Bible about putting new wine in an old wineskin. This means that we cannot take a new thought and put it in an old mind or old habit. Sometimes we have to shed the old to make room for the new.

When I decided to live with God and to be in a daily love relationship with God I had to shed some old skin. I had to re-evaluate my relationships and my quality of life. I had to repent my sins and transgressions. I had to atone for my wrong thoughts and negative actions. And I hate to admit this, but there were a number of negative actions and negative thoughts that I had to take responsibility for.

But once I began my repentance, I discovered Grace and Grace brought me through so that I could have a relationship where I lived, moved and had my being in Christ.

Living with God takes admission of our faults and atonement for having done things wrongly.

Shedding the old takes more time than I had thought it would. It's a process. It isn't like changing a pair of pants or slipping on a new dress. Shedding the old means shaking the old loose from the inside out. That takes hard work, diligence, and complete self-honesty. It can be a painful process, shameful even, and trying – but necessary.

But loving God has shown me that I am human, and I

make very human mistakes yet, through it all He is there waiting for me on the other side of all that I am processing. He is there ready to receive me again.

When I am enjoying this type of a relationship with God, what type of people do you think I am also attracting at this time? Yes, I am attracting people who also love God and want to live a godly life. My friends and my God are not in two separate rooms. We are all living together in harmony.

Atoning for my sins set me free to live a life of

_____

_____

_____

_____

_____

_____

_____

_____

_____

_____

_____

_____

_____

_____

_____

_____

_____

I always thank God for you because of his grace given you in Christ Jesus.

1 Corinthians 1:4 (NKJV)

It Use to be All About Me

IT'S NOT ABOUT ME

I was a selfish person but maybe not in the way one might think. I gave my time, money, and energy to others and to charitable causes, but I was stingy in sharing my heart and life with God. It was all about me and my fleshy desires. Yes, I was doing good in the world, but I was not making time for God – who is my Father and my Creator. Even though I was raised in church and attended Sunday school, I was not available to God.

So, I was selfish in that I thought I had it all figured out.

I began a new Vow to tell myself daily that life was not about me. Life is about the kingdom of God even though at the time I didn't know exactly what that meant. After a few short prayers though, God was sure to inform me that He needed me. This is so very true of all of us. God needs us all to pursue the kingdom as our life journey. God needs us home with Him.

Fleshy desires bring pain and thankfully that is true. For when we are in most pain is when we create the most change in our life. When we are in the most pain, we can be assured we are the furthest from God. My change was that I no longer made my life about me but made my life about God.

I am not saying that I don't have pain in life, but now I have opened the door of my heart to God that gives me peace in all circumstances. There might be problems in

my life, but the pain is far less when I have the peace of
God in my heart.

When I believe that it is all about God
and not all about me I can finally

_____

_____

_____

_____

_____

_____

_____

_____

_____

_____

_____

_____

_____

_____

_____

*To love the LORD your God, and to walk in
all his ways, and to keep his commandments,
and to hold to him, and to serve him with all
your heart and with all your soul.*

Joshua 22:5 (NKJV)

My First Great Grandson

NO MORE BLUE GENES

There is another component to taking up the mantle of God and submitting to a vow with God and that is to model that relationship to others, especially one's own children.

There's an old country song that tells of an overheard conversation the woman's daughter is having with a playmate. The lyrics read, "I don't want to play house because it makes my momma sad." Obviously, the little girl had seen mommy and daddy fighting or mommy crying and didn't want to play a game that her parents had modeled to her to be hurtful. Thank God I never had that in my family!

When we are in a loving relationship with God and we exude the peace and the love of Christ, then we are modeling that to our children as well. They see the God in us. They witness the transformation of us.

I remember a time when I yelled at my daughter after my divorce. I was stressed, tired and going through a major life change. I felt so badly and ashamed for having yelled at her because it certainly wasn't her fault that I was feeling the way I was. It wasn't her fault that I was getting a divorce.

A Day of Change made me want to go to her and apologize for my behavior and ask for forgiveness. That vow meant that I was to take responsibility for my actions.

Parents are not infallible. God is. And God knows this.

Leave a legacy of love to your children by not only entering the vow with Christ, but to model that vow and everything it means to your children.

No more "Blue Genes" is to reverse the sadness and rejection virtually changing our DNA for ourselves, for those around us and for our children.

The way my children can learn about
God through me is to

_____

_____

_____

_____

_____

_____

_____

_____

_____

_____

_____

_____

_____

_____

*And walk in love, as Christ also has loved us,
and has given himself for us an offering and
a sacrifice to God for a sweet-smelling smell.*
Ephesians 5:2 (NKJV)

PLANTED SEEDS

We have heard that we have been endowed with the seeds of greatness. Planting seeds of greatness is surely a good thing. But what exactly makes those seeds grow?

The love and the benevolence of God is what nurtures the seeds of greatness in us and when we look to God as our source and sustenance of existence, our seeds of greatness can blossom to do amazing things in the world.

This is the Vow that God has made to us. When we look to Him, He will be there. When we call to Him, He will come. When we reach out for Him, He will respond.

Planted seeds are hopeful but growing seeds, sprouting seeds are encouraging to our lives and the lives of others.

No one can make our seeds grow like God can. We might think that a relationship can grow our seeds or a job or a new car or a fat bank account, but still, these are all seeds. The only way we can grow into what God has in mind for us is to look to God for nourishment, enrichment, and sustainability.

I have always felt guilty for not nurturing my children as much as I could in their formative years. But that was then. Today I can be more nurturing because God has shown me how. I can give them that nurturing now because God has nurtured me. God and I both can help the seeds of greatness grow in my children and in all those I work with and who I come into contact.

Planted seeds are everywhere and I must believe that every act of kindness and every loving word helps to make the planted seeds in those before me grow.

I know I have been endowed with the seeds of greatness
and how I help those seeds grow is to

_____

_____

_____

_____

_____

_____

_____

_____

_____

_____

_____

_____

_____

_____

_____

*But when the sun came up, the plants were
scorched, and they withered because they
had no root.*

Matthew 13:6 (NKJV)

I KNOW IT NOW

Now my life is one of joy and happiness. I feel very favored to be on the journey. I love to love now! I love to give of myself and of my heart. I love to be a good steward of Christ.

There are many people around me who also are living grand lives and doing good in the world. But they don't know what I know. They haven't figured it out. It's almost like knowing a secret that I want to spill out to everyone.

The secret is that I know now that it is not me that is creating this extraordinary life. People around me still think it is them. They think they have spun the planets of their universe, and everything is moving according to their plan.

Whenever they tell me what wondrous things are going on in their life, I can't help but exclaim, "Praise God!" I know where their good fortune is coming from and one day, I pray they will too.

My background has been that of health, fitness, and eldercare and through caring for people I have met the most extraordinary, most wonderful people ever. And though the circumstances were not perfect and the toll diminished health took on their loved ones was great, I know now that God was with us every step of the way to do and to say what He intended before their life was over. They taught me so much.

We must praise God in both good and bad times. We must praise God in both positive and negative environments. We must simply Praise God!

To think, if you are experiencing favor in your life now, what more could God bestow on you when you acknowledge that He spins the planets and all the circumstances of your life and in Him we find our successes and gifts in life.

I do not begrudge the goodness in other's lives because
I know God has enough favor to

_____

_____

_____

_____

_____

_____

_____

_____

_____

_____

_____

_____

_____

_____

*When pride comes, then comes disgrace, but
with humility comes wisdom.*

Proverbs 11:2 (NKJV)

MAN VS THE ONLY MAN

It is certain that we all long for love. Maybe you have a relationship that perhaps isn't as loving as it once was. Maybe you are between relationships. Maybe you have not been in a relationship for a long while and long for companionship. The truth is, and this is the truth that sets you free, is that there is longing for "a man" and then there is the longing for "The Man."

Which is your desire?

The more I focus on God the more I realize that yes, I do want a man in my life, but the man who has my heart is God. And I know in my relationship with my Father God that He wants that someone special in my life who will adore me, cherish me and love me. I also know that God has already ordered those steps. God has already created the man for me. I don't need to scurry around like a chicken with its head cut off trying to look here, there and yonder for the man who will fulfill my dreams.

So, I look to God, the only man in my life. I look to God as the man in my life who wants me to be loved and happy. I trust in that and that is enough.

When I was down and out in my life, I wanted God to fight for me. I would plead and pray that God fight for me and then it was as if He was speaking right to me when I heard the words, "That's what I've always wanted."

It was so plain. He was fighting for me!

I let go of my seeming problems and turned my heart toward Him. I found contentment. I found peace. I found acceptance. I found Love.

I got the message. God wants us to put Him first and love Him with all our heart, mind, and soul.

The truth that sets me free is that

_____

_____

_____

_____

_____

_____

_____

_____

_____

_____

_____

_____

_____

_____

_____

_____

_____

_____

And ye shall know the truth, and the truth shall set you free.

John 8:32 (NKJV)

FORGIVENESS

I find when I want forgiveness from my friends, I expect to receive it. I expect that my friends will embrace me and let me know that I am loved. But then, when I am asking forgiveness from God I feel that God might hold a grudge or make me earn His favor. This is not our God at all. God forgives us time and time again. But the most unforgiving person I know of that can definitely take me to task is actually, me!

I hold myself in such contempt for the transgressions I have made and for the things I have done. I chide myself for causing others pain and for not being a better example of a Christian.

I am so hard on myself for not being the perfect example of Christ. I am the hardest to forgive myself.

When I am feeling so low about myself, I just sit with God and let Him lead me to still waters. I allow God to ease my mind and to soothe my pain. I allow God to love me and to tell me that He realizes I am not perfect so why can't I realize the same.

It is easy to fall into a depressed state after promising God that He would come first and that my heart was set on Him. I felt ashamed and guilty. I had a hard time forgiving myself, but when I finally would it was as if God was right there asking "What took you so long!"

We do not have to take ourselves so seriously. Do not be hard on yourself. God won't be.

God does not expect me to be perfect
and that makes me feel

_____

_____

_____

_____

_____

_____

_____

_____

_____

_____

_____

_____

_____

_____

_____

*When they came to Jesus, they begged him
earnestly, saying, "He is worthy for you to do
this for him."*

Luke 7:4 (NKJV)

BROKEN VOW

Oh my gosh! Another broken vow! Who am I to talk about the vow with God if I cannot even do this myself.

Here I was sleeping with another man and not married. Playing house. I was giving myself away again. I was betraying God and betraying me.

Here I was again with another man who didn't respect himself and yet, expecting him to respect me – and greater, having us both respect God. I had to stop! My peace was gone, and I wanted it back. I did not want the flesh to win. I wanted to get back to my vow.

To take up the Vow doesn't mean that we are taking up the mantle of perfection. We cannot be perfect. The vow is to imply the relationship and not the behavior. Big difference.

We are not stating that our behaviors will be perfect when we take up the vow with God. When we make a vow with God, we are proclaiming our love for God and our willingness to do right by God. We are making plain and clear that our hearts are united with God.

Just as in a relationship of the flesh, we make mistakes. We hurt feelings and step on toes, but the intent is to truly love that person. Same is true with God.

We are not to focus on the Vow being broken because of our missteps but to know the Vow is constant as we are constantly trying to align our heart with God.

I had to get back with God. So, I ended this relationship and then prepared myself for the man God had intended for me.

Behavior does not equal my intent to love
God and that makes me feel like

_____

_____

_____

_____

_____

_____

_____

_____

_____

_____

_____

_____

_____

_____

_____

My goal in giving you this order is for love to flow from a pure heart, from a clear conscience, and from a sincere faith.

1 Timothy 1:5 (NKJV)

THE FAST

We read in the Bible that many would fast before they made major decisions in their life. I always wondered what one had to do with the other. Why would fasting make a difference? How could fasting make a difference? I had only fasted as a child in Sunday school class, and usually child issues like giving up chocolate.

So, I fasted and just cleared my mind, my system of junk food and junk thoughts. I decided also to fly out to my daughter's home to find my center and to literally put distance between me and him. Wouldn't you know it, I ran into a minister acquaintance of mine. Was it chance or did God know that I was finally receptive to the direction He had for me? There was no doubt that this was of God!

He began to minister to me about relationships and about being equally yoked. Not only did I hear him, but I finally heard that message: Equally Yoked. That was very powerful.

Can you imagine? God so directed this minister to be at the airport precisely when I was there and to be seated right next to me! Was it the fast? I believe it was. Because I was finally ready to listen.

Now I look at relationships differently. I acknowledge what God has given me and then I match that to someone I might be interested in. Do they match my gift and do I match theirs. Are we believers in the same things and the same God? Are we equally yoked?

I cannot say for certain that fasting made the difference. What I can say for sure is that I was willing to surrender food for the thought of God.

To be equally yoked means that

_____

_____

_____

_____

_____

_____

_____

_____

_____

_____

_____

_____

_____

_____

_____

_____

I humbled my soul with fasting; and my prayer returned into my own bosom.

Psalms 35:13 (NKJV)

My Friend and I

THE DECEIVERS

Just as sure as we begin to move in the ways and the will of God, there are those that come to take us off track. Ever heard of the Silver-Tongued Devil? Many people have had such an encounter and both men and women can turn out to be deceivers.

One would think that by expressing my experiences within the folds of this book that I would be so experienced and learned that I could not be easily deceived, but such is not the case.

While writing my first book, I thought I had met a wonderful man whom I will refer to as Doug though this is not his real name. It was important to me that I remained single throughout the writing of the book keeping the vow I had entered into with God. I didn't want the book to sound like "if you do this – then love will happen" as if it were an organic by-product of the book.

I wanted to share that we must make and keep our vow to God to look to Him and to Him Only. However, just as the book was published, I met Doug, and he was just perfect it seemed. I wanted to believe that he was heaven sent. He even agreed to keep the vow along with me – honoring me. So, in my own delusion I thought, "Wow, God is so good to give me this wonderful man at the conclusion of writing this book." I felt like meeting him was my just reward. I took my eyes off God just for a second. Unfortunately, he turned out to be a complete deceiver.

I believe God had me go through this experience so that I could tell the other side of the story. That life is not a neatly wrapped package with crisp ribbons and bows. I suppose that I fell into that line of thinking, but this is where the Ultimate Deceiver wants us to be. Satan is slick and wants us to take our eyes off God. Satan wants us to fall so completely head over heels in love to the point that we are actually making something fit that is just not right for us. When Doug asked me to marry him, I remember responding, "Are you kidding me?" I knew it did not feel right, but I tried to make it fit. So, I am confessing to you.

I met this man, became engaged and quickly married soon after. I thought that this was divine, and that God's Grace had landed upon my heart gifting me this man. He seemed educated, successful and seemed to know more about God than I did. We prayed together. We went to church together. He was God-loving and appeared to be everything I wanted, but once in the marriage his past caught up with him and his old habits surfaced. He left me the first week of marriage. I mean, he completely abandoned me! He said he was going to a meeting and then never returned. I felt beyond hurt. What he was really doing was visiting other women he had previous relationships with.

The other women knew nothing of me, and I knew nothing of them, but he was essentially "married" to all of us. He played us all! Of course, God is magnificent in that He will reveal to us the crooked places that, with His help, will be made straight. Several months later I met one of the women he had been with. She had ordered my book. She called me and asked if we could meet. We did and found out that we really liked each other, and we have since become good friends and have been able to soothe each other's soul. We actually share our story speaking together hoping and praying others will come to Jesus.

I remember when he left, I wanted to die! I remember falling to my knees and saying, "God, I don't know what is going on, but I do know this is going to be hard and I need you right now." After that I fell asleep. It was like God knew I needed the rest to prepare for what was going to happen next. He wanted me to trust Him and Him alone though the pain seemed unbearable.

But to the lesson.

The lesson is this. Just because we are taking the right steps, things will not magically work out. Just because we are good people, God-loving people, does not mean that we are protected from those who wish to harm us. As long as we have free will, there will be those who will try to take us off course and if our eyes and hearts are not on Him – then we will be deceived.

Of course, I prayed for direction at the time I met this man, but I prayed believing that this relationship was God inspired. In retrospect, I feel the lesson itself was God inspired so that I could spare my reader from thinking that

I was able to ride off into the sunset on a white stead with the man of my dreams.

I find that I am still a work in progress and that through everything God still loves me. My eyes stayed on Jesus. He took me out of the relationship quickly and moved me forward. Jesus embraced me. Ultimately, God told me that I passed the test. I passed the test and came back to Him immediately.

I still continue to look to Him that gives me life everlasting, and I am still dedicated to the vow I made in Him.

There are those that wish to take my eyes off of God. They want me to focus on their needs and their dreams. I must keep my self-focus and my focus on God. I can do this every day by

_____

_____

_____

_____

_____

_____

_____

_____

_____

_____

_____

_____

_____

_____

Listen to my voice in the morning, Lord. Each morning I bring my requests to you and wait expectantly.

Psalms 5:3 (NKJV)

VOW TO SELF

Maybe the vow to self is the foremost vow to make. I am not saying that the vow to God is not the ultimate for it is, but first we must make a vow to ourselves. How can we think of giving ourselves to God if we feel lowly and less than? Would God want to be in a relationship with someone who feels bad all the time about themselves? I remember being that kind of a person before my divorce. A pretty mixed-up girl.

Think about it. Would you want to be in a relationship where every moment we heard our partner complain about everything under the sun, how they are not pretty enough, good enough, talented enough and so on? No. We want to be in a relationship with someone who feels good about who and what they are. Same is true of God. God doesn't want us to look at what we think we are lacking. God wants us to see His creation in us. God wants us to feel good about who and what we are and not compare ourselves to others.

When we feel good about ourselves, then we feel accepting of God's love and God's favor. How can we ever accept God's good if we feel so bad all the time?

This is where the renewing of the mind came about. In the quiet moments I had to find the person inside that God loved so much and to bring that person to the fore of my life.

So, the first vow is to know that you are worth it: that you are loved and loveable; that you are worthy and valued; that you are a creation of our Most High God and He loves you and wants you. I had a lot of growing up to do. To be alone with God was how I learned to love myself - to respect myself. To know I may be alone with God for the rest of my life and believe Him for my future is all I need. He will deliver my path differently if He chooses. So, I vow to follow Him! To give my whole life to Him!

This is the first vow.

If I don't love myself then no one will.
So, I tell myself daily that

_____

_____

_____

_____

_____

_____

_____

_____

_____

_____

_____

_____

_____

_____

_____

_____

And God saw that it was good.
Genesis 1:10 (NKJV)

NEVER TAKE YOUR EYES OFF JESUS

If there was ever a single-most directive for how to live one's life it would be to never, never, never take your eyes off of God. I find that any time I do, I am stepping all over myself and yet in God's benevolence, He brings me back to the place where I can experience the peace and calm of Him.

But we must realize in all things in this world, there is a daily struggle between God and the Evil Doer. Every day we are called on to make decisions that keep us in obedience with the plan God has set before us and every day Satan tries to take us off course. The only way we can stay on course is to seek God in all ways and to never take our eyes off of Him.

Sometimes, we want things so badly that we begin to contrive that this is what God had in mind. We delude ourselves thinking that what we have created God has ordained. I think this is what I did. At the end of this book, I entered into a relationship that appeared on so many levels to be the relationship God had in store for me at long last. I was elated with this new man in my life, and we moved very fast towards an engagement and marriage. At every corner it seemed like this was God-ordained and I was so thankful that I had this wonderful man in my life. In my mind I wanted it all to work. I mean, what a perfect ending really - to finish my book and to find my everlasting love.

We met at church. Score 1. He was romantic. Score 2. He was Godly. Score 3. He wanted to honor me as I had written about in my book. Score 4. He proposed to me in front of this gorgeous fountain in front of our church. Bonus Point!! Ha. He was doing everything just the right way. He even signed up and paid for a mission trip we scheduled to make together which mesmerized me and I could hardly believe that everything was working out so smoothly. But I was not looking at the whole picture and I was not really seeing into this man, but he clearly saw into me and my vulnerability. Satan was very happy.

And I have to admit, it wasn't his fault. It was my own and I suffered though I learned a very important lesson. The vow I entered into with God was for all things in my life. The vow was for me to trust God in all ways that concerned my life.

I have learned that I must honor my vow by keeping dutiful counsel with God. I go to Him for all things. Each day I am brought closer to God. I realize that all the trials of my life lead me straight back to God and in Him, I am home.

When I find that I am looking to man instead of
looking to God, I remind myself that

_____

_____

_____

_____

_____

_____

_____

_____

_____

_____

_____

_____

_____

_____

_____

_____

_____

*You will keep in perfect peace him whose
mind is steadfast because he trusts in you.*
Isaiah 26:3 (NKJV)

ABOUT THE AUTHOR

Helen loves to read, write, travel, dance and be outdoors. She loves music and working out. Helen also loves spending time with her children, grandchildren, great-grandchildren and friends. Most of all, she loves the Lord with all her heart. Helen's career has spanned working with the elderly, the sick, the handicapped. Helen was born in an Iowa farming community and now lives in Texas with her husband Michael.

Printed in the USA
CPSIA information can be obtained
at www.ICGtesting.com
LVHW010530310524
781682LV00002B/178